Life
Journey

Life Journey

A call to Christ-centred living

To Jean,
With every blessing,
Mary Fleeson

LINDISFARNE
SCRIPTORIUM

Mary Fleeson

First published by Eagle Publishing in 2004, ISBN: 0 86347 516 7

This third edition published by:
Lindisfarne Scriptorium Limited,
Farne House, Marygate,
Holy Island of Lindisfarne,
TD15 2SJ, United Kingdom.
www.lindisfarne-scriptorium.co.uk

ISBN-13: 978 0 9561402 0 3

British Library Cataloguing in Publication Data. A catalogue record for this book is available from the British Library.

Typeset by Lindisfarne Scriptorium Limited.
Book production and preparation by Burning Light Solutions Limited.
Printed and bound in China.

This book is dedicated to Mark, my wonderful husband & Aurian, my beautiful daughter.

Contents

Foreword

by Dr Michelle Brown, formerly Curator of Illuminated Manuscripts at the British Library, including the Lindisfarne Gospels, now part of its Regional Programme.

Invitation

The Unknown Destination   A Call to Journey

Chapters

Each chapter contains a poem, design notes, a suggested activity, a prayer and in many a meditation and Bible quotations.

Follow Him	A Call to Follow
Light Eternal	A Call to Believe
Your Breath	A Call to Travel
Magnificat	A Call to Humility
As the Touch	A Call to Vulnerability
Show Me	A Call to Obey
ACTS	A Call to Pray
Star	A Call to Trust
Tree	A Call to Reconciliation
Graceful Trinity	A Call to Wholeness
Heart	A Call to Confidence
Life Journey	A Call to Togetherness

Foreword

Mary Fleeson lives on Holy Island (Lindisfarne) with her husband, Mark, and daughter, Aurian. Mary and Mark came to the island to live God-centred lives within the small community there. The haunting, windswept landscape of Holy Island, with its sandbanks, dunes, pebble-strewn beaches and grasslands (a haven for wildlife and seabirds, whose incantations soar through the clear air), will stay with you forever once it touches you. The rhythm of the tides which, twice each day, sever the island calf from its mother mainland, dominate life and remind us of the natural constraints upon human will and action. In a 24-hour society such reminders can be all too rare. And yet, this alone is not what singles out Holy Island as special. It is, surely, the cumulative holiness of the place; hallowed since the foundation of its first monastery, by Irish monks from St. Columbas' Iona, in 635. The prayers of outstanding people such as Saints Aidan and Cuthbert entwine, like interlace, with those of the pilgrims who flock there still, seeping into the soil and the very stones of the places of worship.

Labour has also been a perpetual feature of the island's life. The early monks lived a simple, ascetic life - sustained by prayer and by opus dei (their work for God). In this they were joined by the 'people of St Cuthbert', the islanders who farmed, fished and traded there. Even bishops and abbots tempered their humility by hard manual labour. One, Bishop Eadfrith (died 721), carved out time from his busy schedule, over a number of years, to produce one of the most beautiful expressions ever seen of the unity of Creation and its relationship with the Creator, the Lindisfarne Gospels. He undertook this gruelling physical and intellectual feat as an act of prayer and praise on behalf of all, like St Cuthbert doing battle with his demons on the Inner Farne hermitage nearby. They both balanced the active and contemplative, juxtaposing the needs of the world with those of eternity and acknowledging the need to retreat from the world in order to be filled with the Spirit, and the energy, to re-enter and work for 'the kingdom' within it.

Mary's creativity reflects all these strands, in her vibrant organic images, her scribal work, her words, her drama and dance. Travelling alongside her family, friends and community, she recognises that she has her own unique journey, as do we all. Her gifts are such that she is able to share it with us through her work, and help us all on our way. Thank you, Mary.

Dr Michelle Brown, formerly Curator of Illuminated Manuscripts at the British Library, including the Lindisfarne Gospels, now part of its Regional Programme.

The
Unknown
Destination

A Call to
Journey

A Call to Journey

My journey is always just beginning.
A fresh new day,
On an old, old path.
That's the blessing,
That's where the hope blossoms
However much I wandered yesterday
I can start again tomorrow
And when all my tomorrows are used up,
I'll still have travelled
And you know what people say,
It's the Journey that counts,
Not the arriving.

A Call to Journey An invitation

Dear Reader,

You are invited to accompany me on a journey, to share a quiet walk, some thoughtful moments and a few challenges.

The aim of this book is simple. I hope that through the imagery and words that you are drawn closer to the God that inspired them.

This is not a book of answers. I only hope to share with you a little of what I have discovered since becoming a Christian and encourage you to ask questions of yourself, of others and of God. Ask God for the right questions to ask and be open to challenging your preconceived ideas.

Please enjoy the artwork, it has all been created on the Holy Island of Lindisfarne in Northumbria, inspired by God and the beautiful surroundings (some people say that Holy Island is a 'thin place', somewhere you feel that you can reach out and touch God); read about my thoughts on the Journey, I hope that you will find some things to make you think and some things to make you feel that you have a companion on your Journey; please try the suggested activities on your own or with a small group and when the time is right pray the prayers.

14

The design of 'Journey' was an experiment inspired by a manuscript at the British Library. The parchment I saw, had been painted with a rich purple-red ink and the script was formed using gold ink which appeared coppery in colour. Therefore I formed my cross in a similar way and to achieve the layered textural depth effect I experimented with collage.

The working title for the piece was 'Unknown Journey', its layers representing C.S Lewis' view of death as an 'onward and upward' journey to a better, brighter, more 'real' place.

My
Prayer
for
you

I pray that God will speak loudly
And that you will hear humbly.

I pray that God will act mightily
And that you will receive graciously.

I pray that God will bless amazingly
And that you will share freely.

I pray that God will be close
And that you will walk safely.

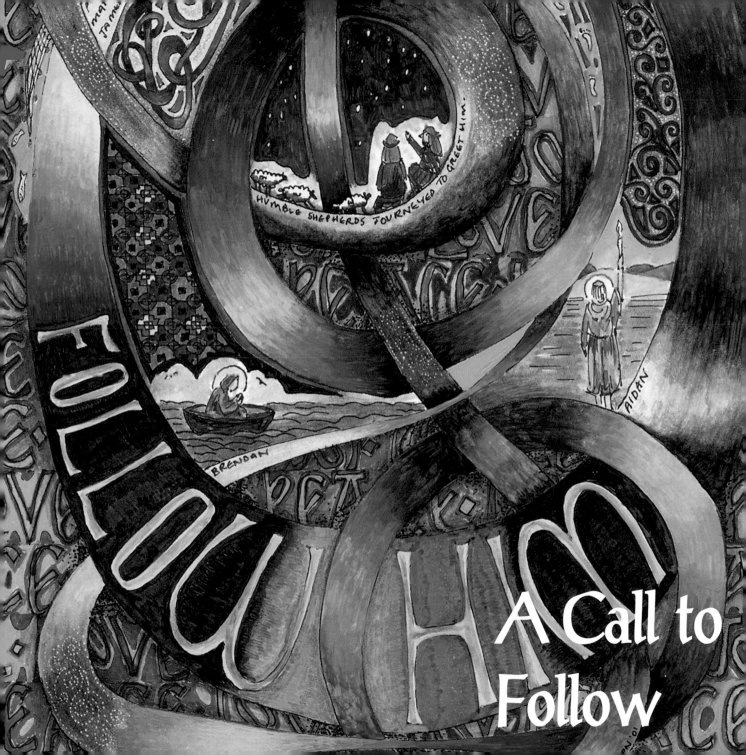

A Call to Follow

I follow Jesus
Who is man, human, whole, impartial,
Passionate,
Curious
And yet also God, incarnate, creative and created
            To walk beside us.
      I follow the Shepherd
            Like a lamb, trusting, comforted, safe,
            Held in a strength
            Beyond my own.
      Knowing that I am sought, special, precious
            And enabled to be.
      I follow the saints,
            Those who followed Him before,
            Those who died
            To self, For Him,
      I learn from their lives, sacrifice and wisdom.
            God given.
I follow because
      I am called, desired, loved and cherished
      By my Creator,
      My Saviour.
Asked only to love in return, love others
            And be loved.

A Call to Follow

We are called to follow Jesus and in doing so we become subject to His teaching and God's commands, with help from the Holy Spirit we are given grace to become more like Him.

The call to follow Him is beyond the human limitations of masculinity or femininity. Jesus, whilst being wholly male, brings salvation equally to men and women, slaves and free, Jews and Gentiles, the body He was born into was not as important as the message it bore. Although He was born a male Jew who was single, trained as a carpenter and travelled around teaching, that does not mean that we have to be the same to be loved by God or be saved. Jesus taught by example, He showed us that He was passionate about honouring His Father by turning the money-changers out of His Father's house, that He was able to resist temptation even when He was offered the world and that He was compassionate even to those who the rest of the community considered outside society such as lepers and prostitutes. All these attributes are attainable by everyone through grace..

How others have followed Jesus' example can also give us valuable tips on how to do the same.

Zacchaeus' story shows us the transforming power of God's love. Jesus showed unconditional acceptance of Zacchacus as a sinner and Zacchaeus, once validated, changed.

Saul, who became Paul, needed a bright light and God's voice from the sky before he changed completely, most of us are not powerful leaders with a vendetta against a particular portion of society but our changes need be no less profound, we can become so much more, so much closer to our Creator God through His transforming love.

The disciples were so convinced by Jesus that they were willing to leave everything to follow, they were willing to take on the urgency of Jesus' mission even to the point of leaving before a beloved father had been buried. They continued Jesus' passion and dedication, even after the crucifixion, through many trials and hardships.

Aidan, under God's direction suggested that the Northumbrians, rather than being treated as heathen barbarians who needed to be saved as quickly as possible through large doses of preaching and Christian discipline, should have the gospel presented as you would give milk to a baby, by the gentle example of working alongside them. Aidan's actions teach us tolerance, patience and great humility, he laid aside his own will and allowed God complete control.

Brendan was a monk from Ireland who was willing to set sail in a coracle, a small, relatively flimsy boat and go wherever God would take him, wherever the winds and currents would direct him, trusting that God would teach him and lead him to the place he was needed most. It is said that he landed on the coast of America

but the landing is not so important in this case as the journeying. Brendan was willing to just go wherever God led, willing to sacrifice all, even his life on this earth.

Each of us has a call to follow Christ's teaching, accepting that call unreservedly enables us to fulfil our potential, to become the person God has created us to be.

'Follow Him' was inspired by the lives of ordinary men who became extraordinary by the act of following when God called.

I chose rich, royal colours to represent the weaving of their life stories and to symbolise the origin of the calling to follow the King of Kings wherever He may lead.

In this piece I imagined that I was constucting visual music, a composition with a steady background beat or refrain (the repeated words, 'love', 'joy' and 'peace' behind the main imagery) and a flowing tune with light and shade in the complexity of the knotwork.

The little figures are the ballads which tell the story of the music, little airs which add depth and tone.

As he neared Damascus on his journey, suddenly a light from heaven flashed around him. He fell to the ground and heard a voice say to him, 'Saul, Saul, why do you persecute me?'

After Jesus was born in Bethlehem in Judea, during the time of King Herod, Magi from the east came to Jerusalem and asked, 'Where is the one who has been born king of the Jews? We saw his star in the east and have come to worship him.'

When the angels had left them and gone into heaven, the shepherds said to one another, 'Let's go to Bethlehem and see this thing that has happened, which the Lord has told us about.'

24

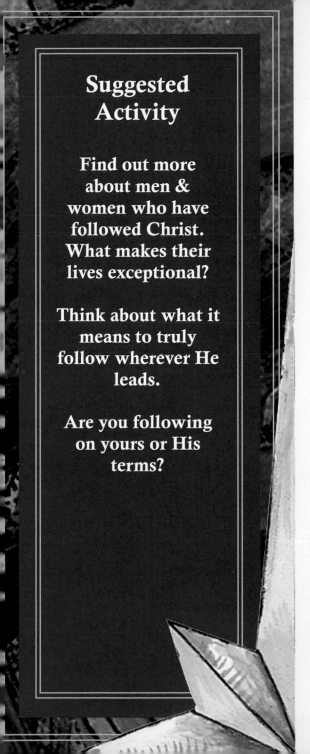
LUKE 19:9-10 Jesus said to Zacchaeus, 'Today salvation has come to this house, because this man, too, is a son of Abraham. For the Son of Man came to seek and to save what was lost.'

MATTHEW 4:19-20 'Come, follow me,' Jesus said, 'and I will make you fishers of men.' At once they left their nets and followed him.

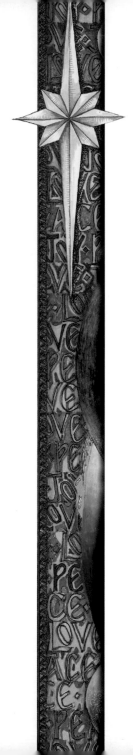

A Call to Pray

As I follow You today Lord,
let me, Your creation
discover how to be creative.

As I follow You today Lord,
let me, Your child
begin to understand how I am precious.

As I follow You today Lord,
let me, Your new saint
learn sacrifice and wisdom.

As I follow You today Lord,
let me, Your beloved
accept love from others
and give love in return.

Light Eternal
A Call to Believe

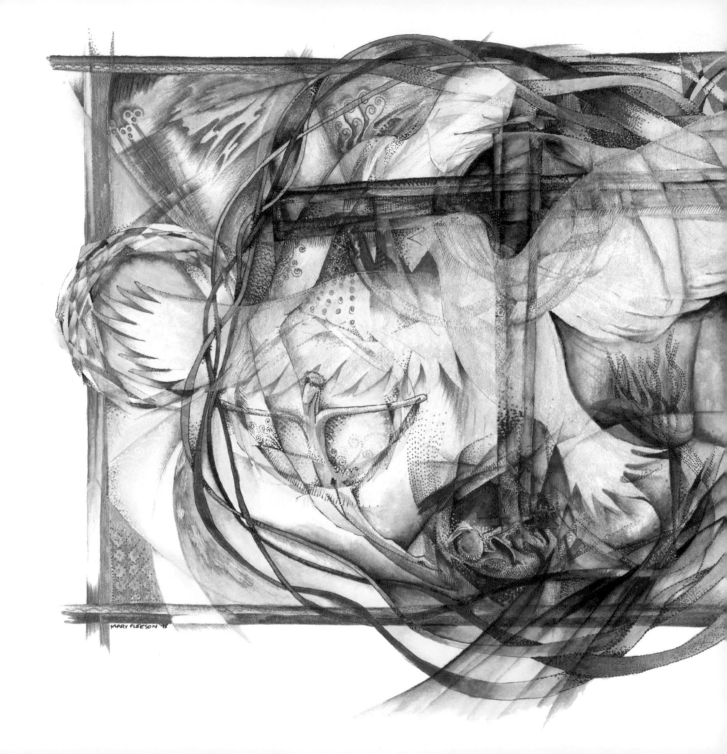

MARY FLEESON '98

A Call to Believe

My Creator, I worship You,
Your immensity surrounds me.
My Saviour I worship You,
Your sacrifice humbles me.
My Light, I worship You,
Your purity overwhelms me.

A Call to Believe

We are called in our everyday life as Christians to believe in the seemingly impossible. In a world which makes little sense we are asked to believe in a virgin birth, our God becoming a man and walking amongst us, a resurrection from death, miracles and creation itself. Like the Queen in Alice in Wonderland who believed as many as 'six impossible things before breakfast' we are challenged to achieve a similar feat!

It is that belief or faith which defines our humanity, and our Christianity by challenging us beyond our perception and sometimes our experience. We cannot know for certain what our limited senses cannot confirm. I cannot 'know' that tomorrow's weather will be sunny or wet because there is no way to experience tomorrow's weather today but I can make a fairly accurate forecast by gathering evidence from people who have many years experience of 'knowing' the weather and I can make a judgement from my own previous experience, Christian belief is very similar. I can be reassured that many experts have studied past evidence (the real experiences others have had of the Trinity), I can listen to others who believe they have had experiences of God and I can identify when my own experiences have been directed by something I cannot easily rationalise. For some that evidence will never be quite enough, they are the people who will always remember the times when the weather didn't behave quite as expected.

I think that perhaps real faith is in the belief that tomorrow will arrive, whatever the weather, and in the same way God is, was and always will be.

Light Eternal is based on an album called Lux Aeterna by David Fitzgerald. I drew together elements from David's inspirations with themes from some of the tracks, such as 'Christchild', 'Golgotha' and 'Resurrection'.

The Trinity is expressed in the embracing figure of God the Father behind the cross, the dove of the Spirit and the representations of Jesus as a babe in the womb and ascending to His Father.

For a fuller explanation of the imagery please visit David's website, address at the end of the book.

1 TIMOTHY 1:17 Unto the King eternal, immortal, invisible, the only wise God, be honour and glory for ever and ever. Amen.

GENESIS 1:1 In the beginning God created the heaven and the earth.

MATTHEW 28:6 He is not here: for he is risen, as he said.

JOHN 8:12 Jesus spoke to them, saying, 'I am the light of the world: he who follows me will not walk in darkness, but will have the light of life.'

JOHN 20:29 'blessed are those who have not seen and yet have believed.'

JOHN 1:14 And the Word was made flesh, and dwelt among us

ACTS 1:8 'But you shall receive power when the Holy Spirit has come upon you; and you shall be my witnesses.'

GENESIS 1:3 And God said, Let there be light: and there was light.

Suggested Activity

Read the following list of words and then consider the main picture two pages back. Which part of the image jumps out at you?

Pray and meditate on that item.

Golgotha
Christ Child
Columcille, Dove of the Church
Transfiguration
Father's Arms
Rainbow
Endless knot of love

A Call to Pray

Lord, help me in my unbelief,
Help my heart to accept what my mind cannot understand.

May my faith be as trusting as a bird on the wing,
      as simple as the beauty of a clear summer sky,
            as sure as the earth beneath my feet.

May I sense the power of creation,
      embrace the sacrifice of love,
            and experience Your healing in my life.

            Lord, thank You for hearing my prayer.

Your Breath

A Call to Travel

Your breath I hear as the wind whispering worship

Your peace I seek as I travel

Your face I see as the sun smiling solace

I seek as I travel

Your peace

Your hand I feel as the water cradling comfort

Your peace I seek as I travel

For the glory of God alone — MF 2000

A Call to Travel

Your breath I hear as the wind, whispering worship.
Your peace I seek as I travel.
Your face I see as the sun, smiling solace.
Your peace I seek as I travel.
Your hand I feel as the water, cradling comfort.
Your peace I seek as I travel.

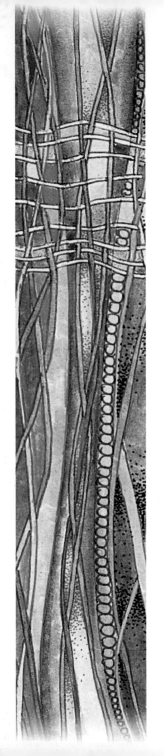

EXODUS 13:21 By day the LORD went ahead of them in a pillar of cloud to guide them on their way and by night in a pillar of fire to give them light, so that they could travel by day or night.

ACTS 8:4 Those who had been scattered preached the word wherever they went.

EXODUS 3:7-8 The LORD said, 'I have indeed seen the misery of my people in Egypt. I have heard them crying out because of their slave drivers, and I am concerned about their suffering. So I have come down to rescue them from the hand of the Egyptians and to bring them up out of that land into a good and spacious land, a land flowing with milk and honey.'

MATTHEW 10:9-10 Do not take along any gold or silver or copper in your belts; take no bag for the journey, or extra tunic, or sandals or a staff; for the worker is worth his keep.

43

Your Breath I hear as the wind Whispering Worship

Suggested Activity

A call to travel is like a call to mission, a call to be willing to go wherever God directs however distant the place and to do whatever God asks when you get there. Many people have sacrificed a home, nearby relatives, financial security and even physical safety to go where they believed God called them.

If you know people who have followed a call to travel, pray for them.

Is God calling you to go somewhere? Spend some time in a quiet place asking God if you are where He wants you to be.

When you next make a journey pray that God will lead you to have significant conversations and that He will bless all your meetings with others and your relationship with those you may be travelling with.

A Call to Pray

Be by my side dear Lord,
Every step I take,

Be before me, dear Lord,
Every step I take,

Be behind me dear Lord,
Every step I take,

Be in me dear Lord,
Every step I take.

Magnificat
A Call to
Humility

MY SOUL
MAGNIFIES
THE LORD
MY SPIRIT
REJOICES
IN GOD
MY SAVIOUR

A Call to Humility

My soul magnifies the Lord
My spirit rejoices in God my Saviour,
By grace You have given me
      Life
      Never ending, eternally in your presence,
      Hope
      Growing, maturing daily, fed by the knowledge of love,
      Joy
      Deep in my soul, defeating sorrow and human pain.

From before my birth You chose me
      To live,
      Each moment nearing fulfilment of my potential,
      To worship
      My Father, my Saviour, My God,
      To serve
      The stranger and friend in obedience and compassion.

A Call to Humility

As I write this I am just a few weeks away from giving birth. The conception was unexpected having spent many years living with the possibility of not having children, my husband and I had quite accepted that being childless was part of His plan for us. I was, therefore, completely unprepared for the range of emotions that would be my companions from the moment I knew.

I have felt, at various times, resentful that my life is about to change so dramatically, ecstatic that God has heard the prayers I'd almost given up praying, frightened that it would go wrong, confused because I'm not happy all the time, overwhelming love for the tiny life inside me, incredible peace and total panic. I've been told that these are the normal reactions of many first time pregnant women (and fathers to be), regardless of age, background or race. Rarely is the woman entirely overjoyed and complacently positive about the experience because our knowledge of the 'things that can go wrong' and our raging hormones conspire to make sure that we behave in a temperate manner to protect the child.

Being aware of my reactions to impending motherhood has made me appreciate the Virgin Mary's life story much more. I'm sure that the Bible wouldn't record all her thoughts and feelings, Mary was born into a culture where women's 'things' were unlikely to be shared with the menfolk, but we are given to understand that she was a normal woman, who was quite young at the time of the annunciation. If that is true then however devout she was she would still have experienced much of the turmoil of feelings that modern mothers feel today. Add to that the knowledge that she is carrying the Son of God!

The Magnificat reveals a strong human with a powerful understanding of her place in God's plan for the world. She is humble without belittling the enormity of God's working in her life and she is mindful of her heritage and the precedence for the God of her forebears lifting those of humble station to positions of undreamt of authority and power.

The figure in 'Magnificat' was designed to be deliberately androgenous so that anyone could confidently repeat Mary's words.

The woven strands rising like incense smoke from the vibrantly coloured figure are prayers coming from all parts of the body to symbolise that prayer is an energetic, body, mind and spirit activity.

The plant drawn behind the wording grows upwards to represent the fruitfulness of a life steeped in prayer and wholly given to God's purpose.

LUKE 1:46-55 And Mary said: 'My soul glorifies the Lord and my spirit rejoices in **God my Saviour**, for he has been mindful of the humble state of his servant. From now on all generations will call me blessed, for the **Mighty One has done great things for me: Holy is his name.** His mercy extends to those who fear him, from generation to generation. He has performed mighty deeds with his arm; he has scattered those who are proud in their inmost thoughts. He has brought down rulers from their thrones but has lifted up the humble. He has filled the **hungry** with good things but has sent the rich away empty. He has helped his servant Israel, remembering to be merciful to Abraham and his descendants forever, even as he said to our fathers.'

1 PETER 10 Each one should use whatever gift he has received to serve others, faithfully administering God's grace in its various forms.

PROVERBS 11:2 ...but with humility comes wisdom.

MATTHEW 22:37-38 Jesus replied: 'Love the Lord your God with all your heart and with all your soul and with all your mind. This is the first and greatest commandment.'

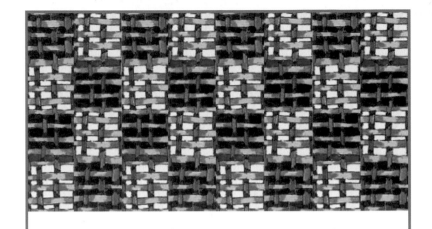

Suggested Activity

Count your blessings!

Really!

Take time to write down the good things in your life at the moment & thank God for them.

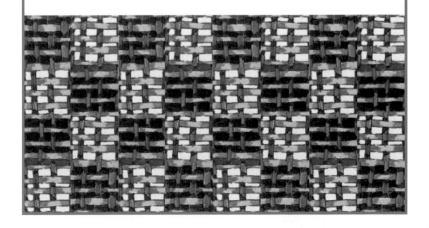

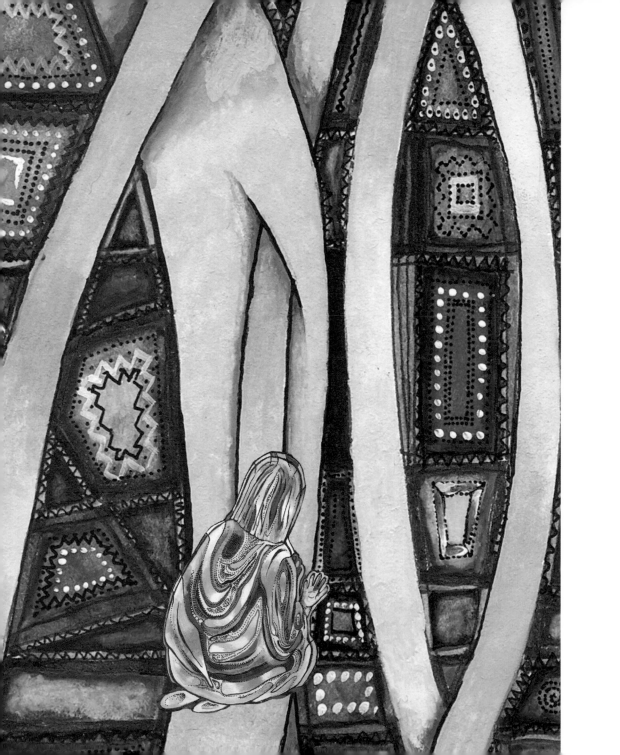

A Call to Pray

Help me to live each moment reaching for the fulfilment of my potential,
Help me to worship You,
my Father,
my Saviour,
my God.
Help me to serve the stranger and friend in obedience and compassion.

I can do nothing without You but with You
I can do anything.

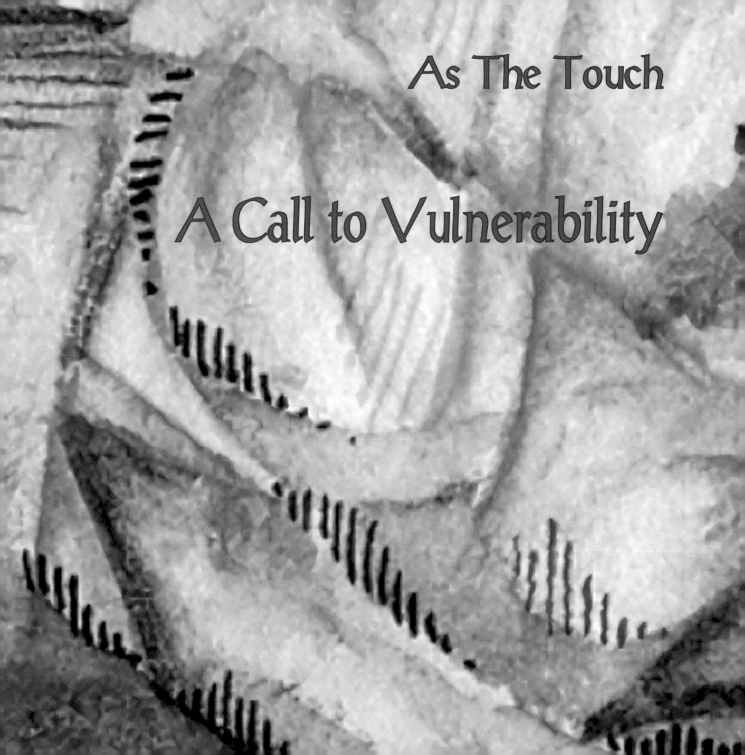

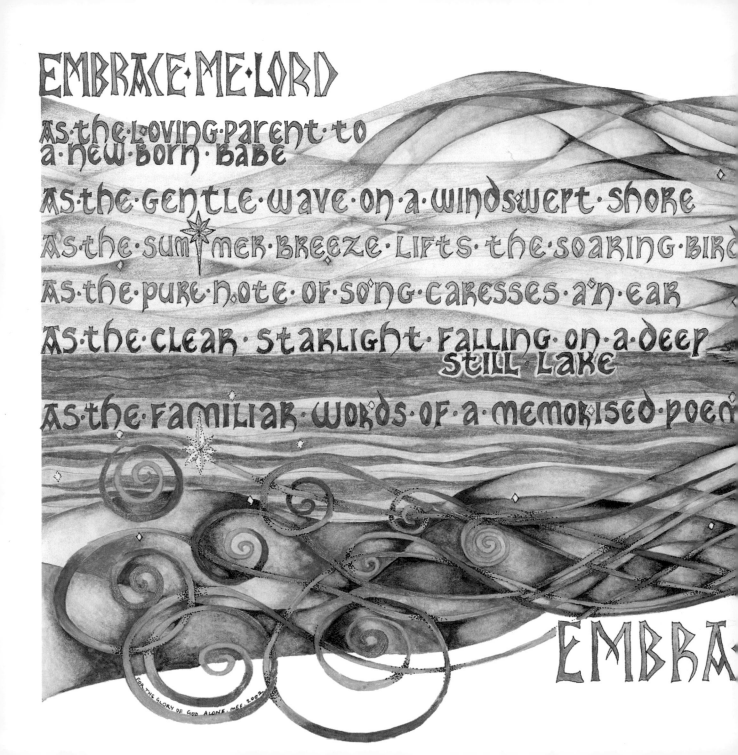

EMBRACE·ME·LORD

AS·the·LOVING·PARENT·to
A·NEW·BORN·BABE

AS·the·GENTLE·WAVE·ON·A·WINDSWEPT·SHORE

AS·the·SUMMER·BREEZE·LIFTS·the·SOARING·BIRD

AS·the·PURE·NOTE·OF·SONG·CARESSES·A'N·EAR

AS·the·CLEAR·STARLIGHT·FALLING·ON·A·DEEP
STILL·LAKE

AS·the·FAMILIAR·WORDS·OF·A·MEMORISED·POEM

FOR·THE·GLORY·OF·GOD·ALONE. MEE 2002

EMBRA

A Call to Vulnerability

Embrace me Lord,
As the loving parent to a new born babe,
As the gentle wave on a windswept shore,
As the summer breeze lifts the soaring bird,
As the fall of rain on the parched garden soil,
As the pure note of song caresses an ear,
As the touch on the face from a lover,
As the clear starlight falling on a deep, still lake,
As the warming sunlight on a butterfly wing,
As the brushstroke on a painter's canvas,
As the soft hug of a much loved toy,
As the familiar words of a memorised poem,
Embrace me O Lord.

A Call to Vulnerability

Originally I intended this section to be 'a call to be comforted' but I realised that to allow yourself to be comforted there is a requirement to be vulnerable to the comforter. To be comforted you have to acknowledge your need to be comforted. You also have to accept that whoever is offering that comfort will not abuse your trust by expecting anything in return or by using their knowledge of your need to their advantage.

Therefore the call is to be vulnerable, to be in a place where we can accept and give comfort and be accountable for our actions in a state which is as near to innocence as is possible for a human.

Vulnerability is a facet of innocence. To be intentionally vulnerable requires us to lay aside defences which we have built to protect our inner self. Our pre-conceived ideas and our selfishness are part of those defensive walls which protect us from the world and can separate us from our Creator God. Vulnerability makes us equal, it makes us childlike and although it may seem to make us weaker in worldly terms it really allows us to become stronger as we allow God to have more of an impact on our lives and allow others nearer to learn from them and be nurtured by them.

If we are to grow in our relationships with others and therefore build a stronger Christian family, we must trust that where our vulnerability may put us in harm's way God will not allow us to suffer alone or to bear what is beyond our ability.

Breaking down our walls does not mean that we relinquish our God given free will, more that we allow our will to be directed by our Creator away from selfish desires and towards a wider purpose.

EMBRACE·ME·LORD

As·the·loving·parent·to
a·new·born·babe

As·the·gentle·wave·on·a·windswept·shore

As·the·summer·breeze·lifts·the·soaring·bird

As·the·pure·note·of·song·caresses·a'n·ear

As·the·clear·starlight·falling·on·a·deep
STILL·LAKE

As·the·familiar·words·of·a·memorised·poem

EMBRACE·ME·O·LORD

The piece 'As the Touch' was initially inspired by the subjects of the poem, the loving parent cradling a baby, waves on a windswept shore, clear starlight and the soaring bird.

I wanted a tranquil blue colour theme with the figures radiating a yellowy light as though reflecting the sun even though the surroundings are in twilight. As the piece evolved I realised that the imagery was speaking of baptism, as sometimes happens God inspired a composition which summarises the subject perfectly. Baptism is defined as 'a first experience of something' and for many God's embrace is like so many new things and always promises the opportunity of a new beginning.

Subsequently the 'soaring bird' became the dove of the Holy Spirit, the parent, stood waist deep in the sea with the baby represent both infant and adult baptism and the golden light radiating from the figures portray the Holy Spirit and the light of Christ, Spirit filled humans bathed in the Son.

1 TIMOTHY 1:15

This is a true saying, and worthy of all men to be received, that **Christ Jesus** came into the world to save sinners.

MATTHEW 11.28

Come unto me all that labour and are heavy laden, and I will refresh you.

Suggested Activity

Think about vulnerability. What does it mean to you today in your everyday life, in your interaction with your family, your friend and strangers? How does it affect your understanding of faith?

Have you surrounded yourself with protective walls which make you think you are invulnerable?

Read the bible verses shown and when you are able, say the prayer on the following page.

If any man sin, we have an Advocate with the Father, Jesus Christ the righteous; and he is the atoning sacrifice for our sins.

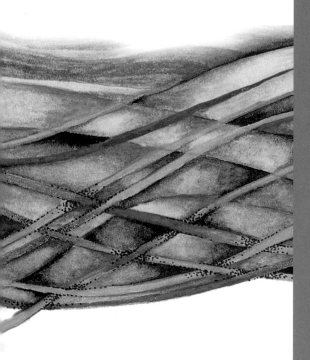

A Call to Pray

Here I am God,
standing/kneeling/sitting before You.
Examine my heart God,
show me Your will.

Here I am Lord,
crying/joyful/fearful before You.
Reveal my need Lord,
show me Your will.

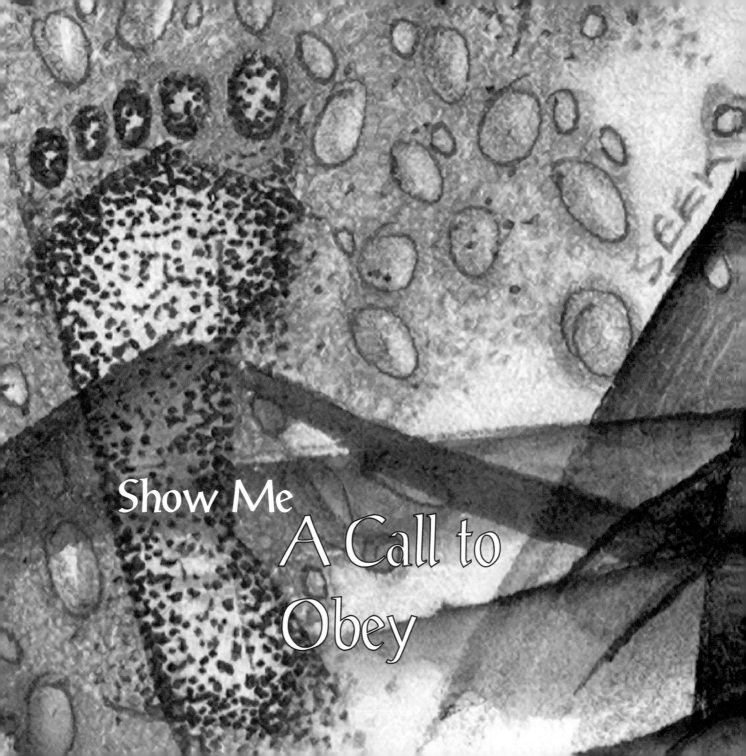

Show Me

A Call to
Obey

A Call to Obey

You say that it is Your blood, shed for me,
I drink and believe in the one true God.
You say I should give to God what belongs to Him,
I give myself and long to return home.
You say that I shouldn't judge others,
I try to see your smile on the stranger's face.
You say that if I am burdened you will give me rest,
I am freed from the stress and the pain.
You said that I should go out to all nations,
I pray I'll be ready for your call.
You said that you would be with me always,
I am peaceful and I am secure.

A
Call
to
Obey

MARK 12:17 Then **Jesus said** to them, 'Give to Caesar what is Caesar's **and to** God what is God's.'

MATTHEW 7:1-2 'Do not judge, or you too will be judged. For in the same way as you judge others, you will be judged, and with the measure you use, it will be measured to you'.

MATTHEW 28:20 '...And surely I am with you always, to the very end of the age.'

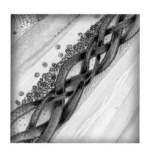

LUKE 22:20 In the same way, after the supper he took the cup, saying, 'This cup is the new covenant in my blood, which is poured out for you.'

MATTHEW 25:37-40 Then the righteous will answer him, 'Lord, when did we see you hungry and feed you, or thirsty and give you something to drink? When did we see you a stranger and invite you in, or needing clothes and clothe you? When did we see you sick or in prison and go to visit you?' The King will reply, 'I tell you the truth, whatever you did for one of the least of these brothers of mine, you did for me.'

ACTS 1:8 'But you will receive power when the Holy Spirit comes on you, and you will be my witnesses in Jerusalem, and in all Judea and Samaria, and to the ends of the earth.'

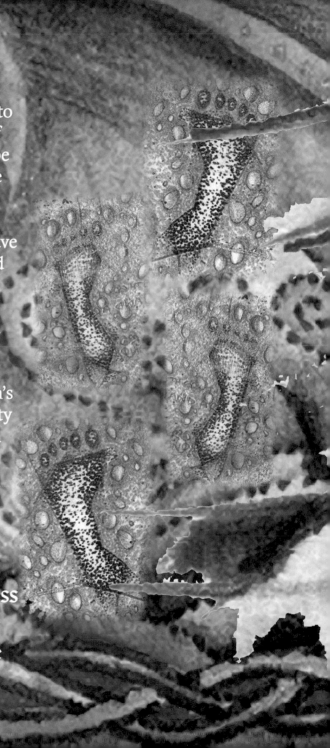

Suggested Activity

Children usually understand that obedience to adults and the rules they impose are part of everyday life and that if they don't want to be punished they have to accept the need to be obedient.

There are occasions when even grown ups have to be obedient, obey the law of the land and for Christians the laws of God.

Ask yourself if you obey rules because you have to or because you want to.

Think about God's commandments and man's rules for society, how do they differ? Is society expected to be obedient to different rules in places which follow different gods?

Why is obedience important? Do we need rules for grown ups?

Jesus said, 'I tell you the truth, unless you change and become like little children, you will never enter the kingdom of heaven.'

A Call to Pray

Precious Lord,

Help me to obey you,
Willingly,
Help me to love,
Unconditionally,
Help me to live,
Kindly,
Help me to help others,
Joyfully,
Help me to praise,
Childishly,

Help me,

My precious

ACTS

A Call to Pray

A Call to Pray

Adore the Lord your God
　　He loves you,
Confess your sin to Him
　　He forgives you,
Thank Him for His mercy
　　He conquered death,
Surrender your desires
　　He is Life.

77

A Call to Pray

When I was a teenager I was part of the lively youth section of a market town Anglican church. One of the first sparks which lit the fire of our group was a series of ecumenical youth Lent meetings led by a charismatic local junior school teacher who was later ordained. He had the ability to bring the Bible to life by telling us how its teaching was being lived out by contemporary Christians, to allow us to question without always giving us pat answers and to encourage us not to be frightened of or dismissive of the power of prayer. He taught us the A.C.T.S. acronym as a way of helping us to structure our prayers, Adoration, Confession, Thanksgiving and Supplication or as I have used, Surrender. The success of the formula is in its longevity of use, twenty years on and I am still using it!

Adoration is a heady and difficult combination of worship, awe and selflessness. In a society where for many the emphasis is on the promotion of self and the concept of worship and awe is reserved for fashion and media stars it can be hard to imagine how to adore something we cannot easily categorise or even describe but the essence of adoration is that it does challenge our limited knowledge and that it takes us outside our limited experience by encouraging us to abandon our self. It is only when we can willingly say to God, 'Without You I am nothing' that we can begin to understand the overwhelming inner peace of adoration.

Confession is something we all have different experiences of depending on our denominational or parental upbringing. James (5:16) suggests that we should 'confess (y)our sins to each other and pray for each other so that (you) we may be healed.' I'm sure I'm not the only person who has found it relatively easy to confess my wilful disobedience to God but painfully difficult to admit to a fellow human that I'm not perfect in every way, but I have learnt that confession isn't about running off a list of misdemeanours so that I can feel better about myself after admitting them but about recognising the shortcomings of my faith and asking God to improve me! One day, after God told me clearly to confess and apologise to someone I had sinned against I realised that my sin was known by God before I even confessed it to Him! Abruptly I was hurled into admitting that God knew me … intimately, my every thought and action, the good AND the bad. After reluctantly obeying God I was aware of the complete peace that comes from releasing my self and trusting that God is right and that I am forgiven. The message was clear, our sin does not only affect those who we sin against but it eats at our soul, masked by our ability to protect our self we see only the minor issues without looking deeper to the sins which have become a way of life.

Thanksgiving is recognising that all good things are from God and that He will give the strength to cope with the bad things and thanking Him regardless of our opinion on what sort of a day we've had. It is counting our blessings, especially when things seem to be going wrong; often if we are weakened physically, mentally and/or spiritually it seems easier to allow ourselves to be lulled downwards to the place where wallowing in self is safe, but if we can pull back from the brink of that cosy pit and recognise that that is not a place that God wants us to be and that there are positive things in our lives, things will improve. All too often we are in the pit before we realise we have stepped over the brink and from that place only God can pull us out. Sometimes then the only prayer needed is 'Help!'.

Supplication or surrendering comes hand in hand with confession, it requires complete submission of body, mind and spirit and constant communication with God. It asks us to trust that our desires and dreams, birthed within that place of complete surrender of self, are placed there by God and will be fulfilled by Him if we trust. Looked at a slightly different way it means that our desires become our calling and our dreams become prophecy, however the emphasis must always be on the complete and willing surrender of self as if selfishness remains then those desires and dreams are liable to corruption.

The design for ACTS aims to focus the viewer's eye on the Adoration, Confession, Thanksgiving and Surrender initials as a visual reminder of the words and to the final line, against the backdrop of a triple stranded plait representing the Trinity, 'He is Life'.

Within each phrase is a small figure, each one in a different aspect of prayer. The first figure has arms stretched upwards in a manner of complete abandonment, its action showing a response to God's love by offering its whole self; the second figure kneels as though at the foot of the cross, asking for and receiving forgiveness; the third is seated in an attitude of contemplation, considering an amazing God; the fourth figure stands with hands dropped to the sides as if saying 'Here am I. Send me!' (Isaiah 6:8).

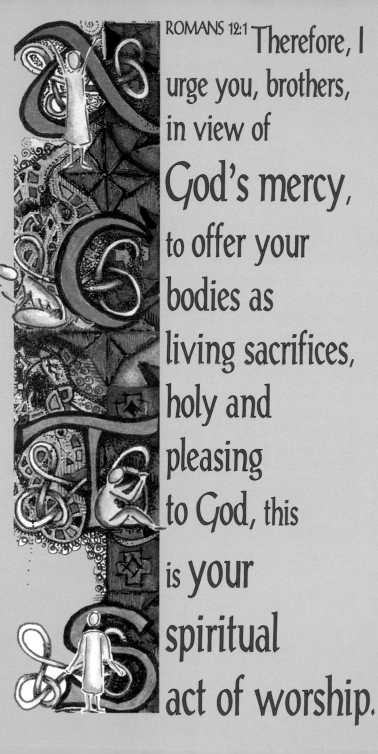

JOHN 3:16 'For God so loved the world that **he gave his one and only Son,** that whoever believes in him shall not perish but have eternal life.'

ROMANS 12:1 Therefore, I urge you, brothers, in view of **God's mercy,** to offer your bodies as living sacrifices, holy and pleasing to God, this **is your spiritual act of worship.**

JAMES 5:16 Therefore confess your sins to each other and pray for each other so that you may be healed.

ROMANS 8:5 ... but those who live in accordance with the Spirit have their minds set on what the Spirit desires.

MATTHEW 5:7 Blessed are the merciful, for they will be shown mercy.

Suggested Activity

Turn back two pages and casually glance at the ACTS piece. What catches your eye? You may notice a word or phrase, an image or pattern, write down or sketch what it is and how it makes you feel. What other things does it bring to mind?

Follow the same exercise with the words opposite.

Pray and think about what draws your attention.

Try and write a prayer based on Adoration, Confession, Supplication and Thanksgiving so:
Praise God
Say you are sorry
Ask God to forgive you
Give thanks for what He has done today

Finally turn the page and read the printed prayer, if you can say the words aloud then stay still for a while, open your heart to what God may want to say to you.

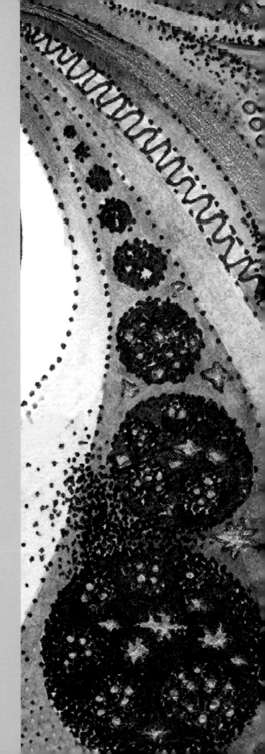

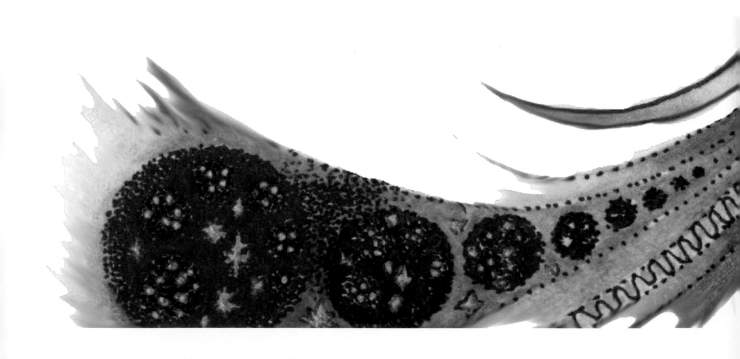

A Call to Pray

With my mind, my body and my spirit
I worship You Lord,
Help me to love You more.
I'm sorry I have made You sad, so many times.
Help me to do Your will.

With my mind, my body and my spirit
I thank You Lord,
Without You I am nothing.
I'm offering You my hopes and my dreams,
Help me to share Your wisdom.

Star

A Call to
Trust

A Call to Trust

Creator God, never ending, eternal, perfect,
    Circle me.
Merciful God, protect and save all those I love
    Circle me.
Awesome God, restore me and keep me safe
    Circle me.

A Call to Trust

The inspiration for Star and Hand is the Celtic tradition of the 'Caim' or encircling, a prayer which combines words and actions (an arm raised with hand outstretched and the body turning in a circle to 'draw' a circle around the body) to ask God to entirely surround and protect the supplicant.

The star describes our Creator God, designer and maker of the universe whom we entrust with our lives. The hand represents humankind reaching out to God in anticipation and confidence. The three linked circles symbolize the Trinity.

It is overwhelming to imagine that the God who inspired the void before creation to become the place where we are now, is the same God who created each one of us, the same God who knew us even in the womb, the same God who gave Himself to save us, the same God who gives us a reason to hope, the same God who trusts us to continue His work on earth.

As supplicants or prayer makers we are not passively asking a distant entity to answer our requests, we are, with the inspiration of the Holy Spirit, actively campaigning for God's will to be done in our lives and the lives of others.

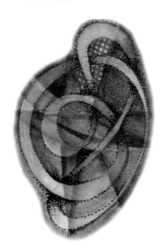

In the simple action of making a circle around ourselves and our lips forming the prayers of our heart with the conscious involvement of our mind we are deliberately combining the agreement of body, mind and spirit with the awesome power of our creator God, trusting that He will answer our petition.

That trust is not a passive, fragile state but an act of joyful passion. It is fervent anticipation and expectation of God's active participation in our life.

'Caim' was originally designed as a CD cover for an album of prayers set to music by the same name, therefore the imagery reflects themes of the music included, however as is often the case the illustration evolved into something which speaks beyond the obvious inspiration.

The hand seems to reach out in a loving, gentle gesture to caress the face of the Creator, symbolised by the star (REVELATION 22:16 'I, Jesus, have sent my angel to give you this testimony for the churches. I am the Root and the Offspring of David, and the bright Morning Star.').

The complex knotwork intersperses three overlapping circles which represent the Trinity and the patterns and colours are life patterns, weaving and merging, coloured by experiences, actions and reactions.

JOHN 14:1-4 'Do not let your hearts be troubled. Trust in God; trust also in me. **In my Father's house are many rooms;** if it were not so, I would have told you. **I am going there to prepare a place for you.** And if I go and prepare a place for you, I will come back and take you to be with me that you also may be where I am. **You know the way to the place where I am going.'**

MARK 3:33-35 **'Who are my mother and my brothers?'** he asked. Then **he looked at those seated in a circle around him** and said, **'Here are my mother and my brothers!** Whoever **does God's will** is my brother and sister and mother.'

Suggested Activity

Think about those people you consider to be your family whether they are related or not.

What can you pray for them today?

Do you know what they really need?

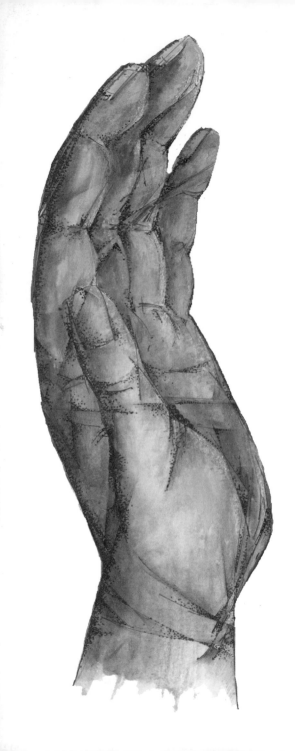

A Call to Pray

Circle me Lord, let love be my reason,
Let hate be a stranger.
Circle me Lord, let joy be my comfort,
Let sadness be no more.
Circle me Lord, let peace be my aim,
Let conflict be resolved.

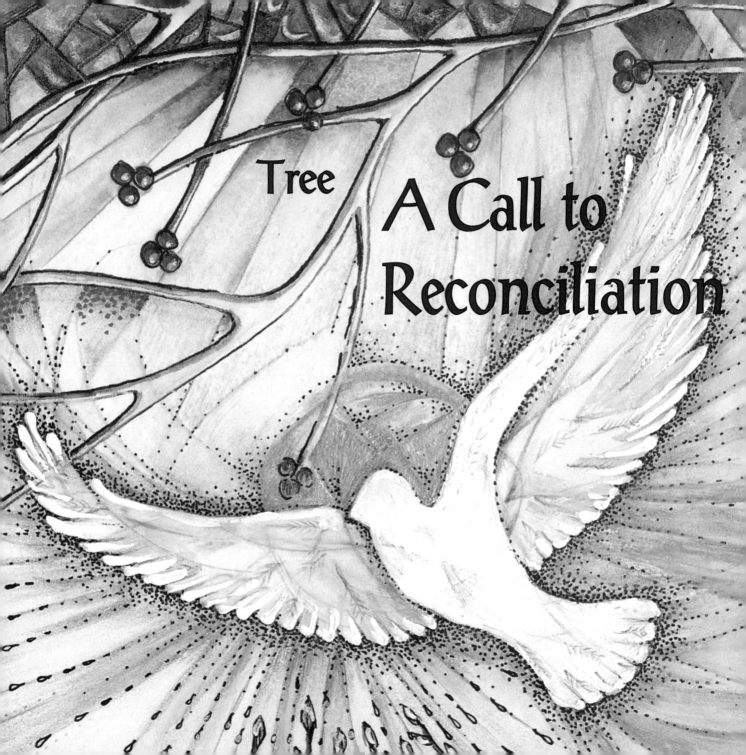

A Call to Reconciliation

If I were Eve in the Garden of Eden
Would I be taken in by a talking snake?
If I were Adam in that Paradise place
Would I risk it all for my partner's sake?
If I were a leader on this garden planet
Would I hear the word 'kill' and obey?
If I were alone, my people all lost
Would I fall to my knees and pray?
If I were living in a land where 'a' hated 'b'
Would I follow the crowd or stop to ask why?
If I were to offer my friendship to another
Would they turn their back or smile and cry!

A Call to Reconciliation

JOHN 1:32 'I saw the Spirit come down from heaven as a dove and remain on him.'

REVELATION 22:2 'On each side of the river stood the tree of life, bearing twelve crops of fruit, yielding its fruit every month. And the leaves of the tree are for the healing of the nations.'

REVELATION 2:7 He who has an ear, let him hear what the Spirit says to the churches. To him who overcomes, I will give the right to eat from the tree of life, which is in the paradise of God.

MATTHEW 26:28 This is my blood of the covenant, which is poured out for many for the forgiveness of sins.

ISAIAH 61:11 For as the soil makes the sprout come up and a garden causes seeds to grow, so the Sovereign LORD will make righteousness and praise spring up before all nations.

JOHN 12:24 I tell you the truth, unless a kernel of wheat falls to the ground and dies, it remains only a single seed. But if it dies, it produces many seeds.

JOHN 19:2 The soldiers twisted together a **crown of thorns** and put it on his head.

GENESIS 2:9 In the middle of **the garden** were the tree of **life** and the tree of the **knowledge** of good and evil.

JOHN 15:5 'I am the vine; you are the branches. If a man remains in me and I in him, he will bear much fruit; apart from me you can do nothing.'

Suggested Activity

Reconciliation can be a painful and difficult action with often insurmountable differences to overcome, its sacrifice and consequence can never be underestimated.

Think about the times when it has been easier to keep enemies rather than find common ground with which to form friendship. Is it too late to change the situation for the better?

Pray the prayer opposite.

A Call to Pray

Healing Lord,
Open the hearts of those in
conflict, help them to receive
your healing.

Merciful Lord,
May our human hearts never
harden to the suffering caused by
the absence of peace, help us to
yearn for peace.

Almighty Lord,
Help us to see where we are
avoiding reconciliation, please
grant us opportunities and the
will to change.

Graceful Trinity

A Call to Wholeness

A Call to Wholeness

Graceful Trinity of love,
Hear our prayer.
You were at the beginning,
You are now, You shall be evermore.
Grant us peace.
With the ebb of the tide,
With the turn of the season,
Grant us peace.
Father, Son and Spirit, Hear our prayer.

A Call to Wholeness

There is a song I've heard which gives a clue about how to understand the concept of the Trinity and therefore the wholeness which is one of the main messages of the Christian faith, it describes a woman who is mother, daughter, wife and sister and a man who is father, son, husband and brother. In each role they fulfil the expectations that the role places on them and some people they interact with will only know them in one of their roles and yet they are the sum of those roles, no less complete if a role were missing but enriched because of the balance of the combination. In the same way an individual is physical, mental and spiritual, needing all three aspects to be a whole person. The Trinity of God the Father, God the Son and God the Holy Spirit is the perfect example of the parts functioning together to enrich the whole.

As the Trinity is a perfect balance, each part complementing the other, so should our relationships balance and complement each other. As Paul said in his letter to the Christians in Rome, each of us has different gifts given at our birth which when placed in the context of a group contributes to the dynamics and effectiveness of that group. These gifts are different to the gifts of the spirit which are given according to our need and personal journey, we cannot request these 'body' gifts, they just are, however, discernment of your innate skills may help you to understand why you 'get on' with some people and jar with others. In any situation which requires teamwork such as families, worship groups, committee, etc. an imbalance of gifting could make life difficult, imagine having all leaders in any group or, perhaps worse, none at all!

God designed us, created each one of us, knew us and blessed us before our birth. He made sure that in the grand scheme of life on the earth we would each have a place, a purpose and a role to play which was essential to the smooth running of humanity. Whether we choose to accept that role or even choose to try and discover what it is, is up to us.

Graceful Trinity was a prayer written to express the omnipotence of the Triune God and His participation in our everyday lives.

I have depicted the four seasons by the changing trees and sun and the daily ebb and flow of a sea which writhes from its depths with activity and life as our lives roll and weave like waves on God our ocean.

JOHN 14:25-26 'All this
I have spoken
while still with you.
But the Counsellor,
the Holy Spirit,
whom the Father
will send in my name,
will teach you
all things
and will remind
you of everything
I have said to you.'

ROMANS 12:4-8 Just as each of us has **one body with many members,** and these members do not all have the same function, so in Christ we who are many form one body, and each member belongs to all the others. We have different gifts, according to the grace given us. If a man's gift is **prophesying,** let him use it in proportion to his faith. If it is **serving,** let him serve; if it is **teaching,** let him teach; if it is **encouraging,** let him encourage; if it is **contributing to the needs of others,** let him give generously; if it is **leadership,** let him govern diligently; if it is **showing mercy,** let him do it cheerfully.

Suggested Activity

Do you know what your gifting is?

There are several ways of discovering your personality type in a Christian context (see the resources page) but generally you can start by understanding that your gifting is determined by who you are and how you instinctively respond to situations rather than by what you do.

Think about how you interact with others and in what situations you feel most yourself, ask yourself why. Then think about situations that make you uncomfortable and ask again why that is.

How can the uncomfortable situations be turned around by being sensitive to other people's gifts?

A Call to Pray

Strong and awesome Father, sacrificial and wise
Son, supporting and restoring Spirit,
        Hear my prayer.
I am small, such a little creature
        and yet I believe that You know me.
I believe that You created me,
I believe that You wanted me ,
        to be part of Your world.
I believe that I have a place,
        a purpose, in Your world,
When that place and purpose is hidden from my
sight please grant me patience and perseverance,
        Don't let me go.
Strong and awesome Father,
        sacrificial and wise Son,
                supporting and restoring Spirit,
                        Hear my prayer.

Heart
A Call to
Confidence

DO NOT BE AFRAID

TO THE GLORY OF GOD STONE—MARY F. 2001.

DO NOT LET YOUR
HEART BE TROUBLED

A Call to Confidence

A pain, deeply buried
(deep cries out to deep),
Our innermost core of being
(He knows the emptiness),
Cracked, torn and barren
(He longs to fill),
Only our vulnerability
(To God and to each other),
Will allow to heal
(He wants to heal you),
His desire is to soothe and protect
(For this He died).

A Call to Confidence

It can be hard to be confident of God's love for us, as humans we find it almost impossible to comprehend that our Creator can have any concern for us as individuals. That He knows each one of us and loves us unconditionally is beyond anything that we can imagine and yet it is true, He does know each one of us, and His desire is to extend that knowledge into a mutual intimacy.

The command, 'Do not let your heart be troubled' challenges us to release the security of our innermost core of being into God's control. Our instinct is to protect ourselves, build up walls between our deepest self and the rest of the world, vulnerability is perceived as weakness because it makes us apparently easy to manipulate, however the walls that we build separate us further from God by shutting Him out too. When we accept the challenge to allow God to protect our heart we allow him to know our soul and direct our desires toward His plan, that way we can fulfil our potential and become the people He created us to be.

The rainbow in the picture represents God's covenant with man, to never again destroy His creation. It is a marvellous symbol, not just of visible renewal and promise but also of the renewal and promise beyond what we can see, it has colours within its structure which are invisible to the naked eye and all the colours combined will become the purest white light and so the rainbow becomes also a symbol of purity and light.

In the context of the call to be confident the rainbow is a reminder of God's promises including the promise to send us a guide, the Holy Spirit, who we can call on at any time.

The dove is like freedom, it shows us how we can be if we accept God's love, it also speaks of the peace we can know if we allow him to direct our lives.

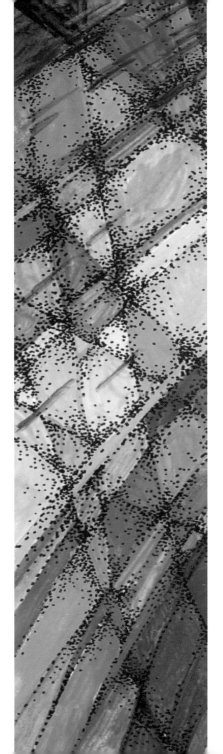

The rainbow has always been a very positive image to me. It is the sunshine through the rain, the vibrant unexpected colours against a familiar background of green, grey, blue and brown, like a summer flower garden in the sky.

It is a happy and wondrous thing and its blessing compliments the words 'do not be afraid, do not let your heart be troubled'.

The dove, an international symbol of peace, is also recognised as the Holy Spirit, the guide and companion sent to us by God to help us not to be afraid or troubled.

GENESIS 9:13 'I have set my rainbow in the clouds, and it will be the sign of the covenant between me and the earth. Whenever I bring clouds over the earth and the rainbow appears in the clouds, I will remember my covenant between me and you and all living creatures of every kind. Never again will the waters become a flood to destroy all life. Whenever the rainbow appears in the clouds, I will see it and remember the everlasting covenant between God and all living creatures of every kind on the earth.'

MATTHEW 3:16 As soon as Jesus was baptized, he went up out of the water. At that moment heaven was opened, and he saw the Spirit of God descending like a dove and lighting on him.

118

PSALMS 42:7 Deep calls to deep in the roar of your waterfalls; all your waves and breakers have swept over me.

LUKE 4:18 'The Spirit of the Lord is on me, because he has anointed me to preach good news to the poor.'

JOHN 14.1 'Do not let your hearts be troubled.'

Suggested Activity

What is troubling you today?

Find enough pebbles so that you have one for each trouble and naming the trouble place its pebble at the foot of a small cross (a stand up one or a picture).

Build the pebbles into a cairn around the cross, you can do this over several days.

As you place each pebble say: 'Today Lord, [*say the trouble*] is worrying me. I give it to You, help me to see with Your eyes and be calm.'

Imagine that each pebble is building a step which you can climb, the more steps you climb the nearer you get to the cross and the closer you get to Jesus' comfort.

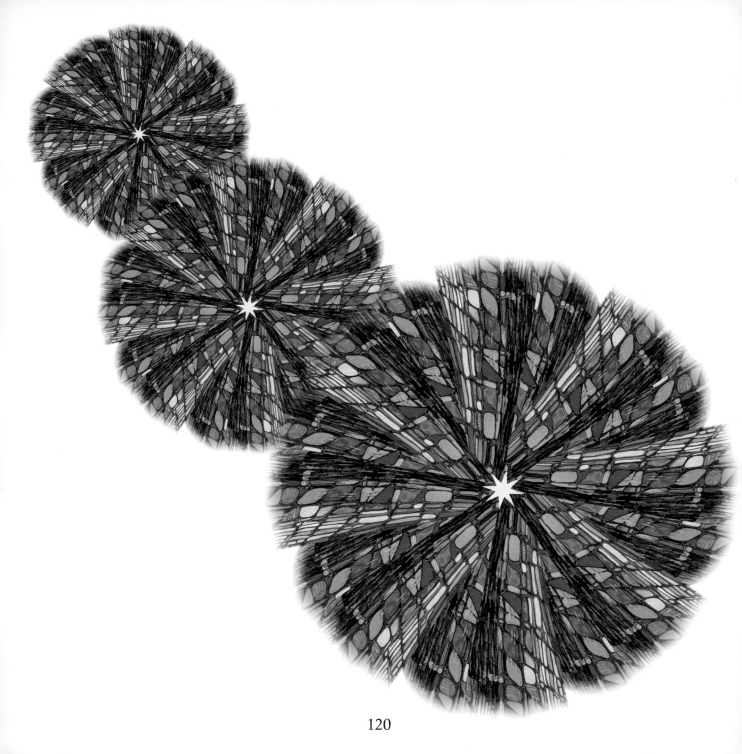

120

A Call to Pray

When all seems black,
help me to remember the peace of Your promise,
When all seems dark,
help me to remember the purity of Your light,
When all seems hopeless,
help me to remember the comfort of Your words,
When all seems discord,
help me to remember the harmony of Your creation.

Life Journey

A Call to
Togetherness

life journey
winding
patterns overlapping
weaving community
touch as you pass smile
hold the moment
as God holds you
in his
heart

A Call to Togetherness

Life journey winding,
Patterns undulating, overlapping
Weaving community.
Touch as you pass, smile,
          hold the moment
As God holds you
          in His heart.

A Call to Togetherness

The weaving of lives in community are expressed in 'Life Journey'. It is about living each moment, making a positive difference in the lives of others and getting to know God better as we meet Him in those we meet.

Look closely at any of the carpet pattern pages in the Lindisfarne Gospels, follow the intricate weaving of the lines, the way that each line complements and supports its neighbour until the finished pattern is an amazing three dimensional weaving. Our lives are like that woven pattern, sometimes our strand of life cord will lie parallel to another for a long time but more often it will cross briefly and offer support or be supported by another person's strand.

In the constant interaction of our life strands we build a pattern of community where mutual support and companionship is tempered by space to explore alone and the completed pattern is both structured and free.

Teresa of Avila reminds us that we are called to be the body of Christ on earth. Each time we meet someone, we are called to see, hear and touch them with the love and wisdom of Christ. To see Him in the stranger, to hear Him, to go to Him and to touch Him we need to be vessels filled by His presence, allowing Him to show God's unending love to and through us.

It is a two-way exercise enabling us to experience God's love and enabling others to experience that love through us.

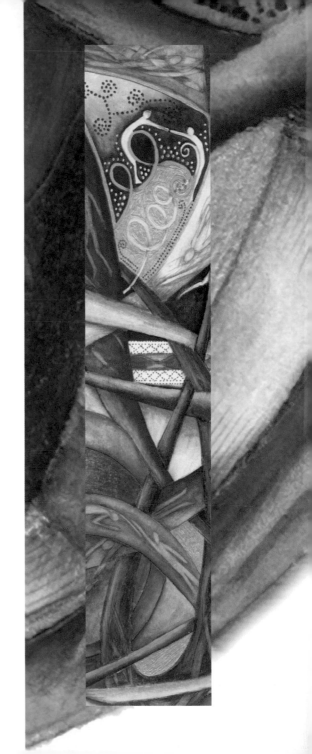

126